# ABE LINCOLN
## President for the People

By Yannick Oney

**World Discovery History Readers™**

SCHOLASTIC INC.

New York • Toronto • London • Auckland • Sydney
Mexico City • New Delhi • Hong Kong • Buenos Aires

*A. Lincoln*

Lincoln was tall and thin, and had a face with
strong features.

# CHAPTER 1

## Young Abe

Abraham Lincoln was born February 12, 1809, on a cold morning at Sinking Spring Farm in Nolin Creek, Kentucky. Abe's parents, Tom and Nancy Lincoln, and Abe's two-year-old sister, Sarah, weren't thinking about the cold. They were busy looking at baby Abe. They didn't know that he would grow up to be a great president.

Abe's father was a farmer. He loved to tell stories. He never learned to read or write very well, but Abe's mother did. She was a kind and cheerful woman who believed in hard work, and was also very religious.

Log cabin where Abraham Lincoln was born

When Abe was two years old, his family moved a few miles away to Knob Creek Farm. This new land was easier to farm.

Abe and Sarah had a lot of work to do on the farm as they grew up. Abe carried water in buckets from the creek. He collected firewood. He helped his father plant seeds in the fields.

In 1809, when Abe was born, the United States had only seventeen states. Kentucky had been a state since 1792. But in 1803, the United States made the Louisiana Purchase. This added land from the Mississippi River to the Rocky Mountains.

A log cabin in Kentucky, near where Abe lived.

There weren't many neighbors near the Lincolns' farm. For fun, Abe would go fishing or swimming in the summer. He set traps to catch rabbits and other animals that his mother would later cook for dinner.

Abe and Sarah went to a one-room schoolhouse about two miles from their home. There weren't many school supplies. Children often used a piece of charcoal on a board to practice their writing. Sometimes Abe and Sarah could not go to school because they were too busy helping their parents on the farm. When Abe wasn't in school, his mother taught him to read and to spell. In fact, all the days that Abe went to school equaled less than one year.

A one-room schoolhouse and outhouse

When Abe was seven, his family left Kentucky. Part of the land that Abe's family lived on was taken from them, because his father could not prove he owned it.

As a boy, Abe spent many hours reading and learning by fire and candlelight.

The family moved to Little Pigeon Creek in southern Indiana. It took the family two weeks to travel to Little Pigeon Creek.

Another reason the Lincolns moved from Kentucky to Indiana was because they did not believe in **slavery**. People could own **slaves** in Kentucky, but not in Indiana. Abe's family belonged to the **Baptist Church**. The Baptist Church did not accept slavery, either. Like the Lincolns, many poor farmers disagreed with slavery.

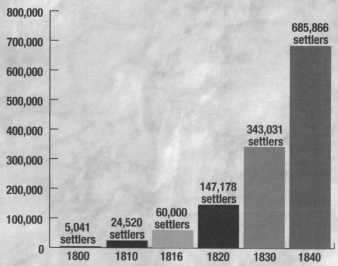

In 1816, Indiana became the nineteenth state. In the early 1800s only Native Americans and a few settlers lived in Indiana. It was a wilderness filled with trees and wild animals such as bears and cougars.

Farmers are clearing land for planting by using ox and horse teams to plow and pull stumps. The Lincolns cleared their land in the same way.

There was a lot of work to do. The land had to be cleared and a house needed to be built. Abe became very good at swinging an ax. For a short while, the Lincolns lived in a shelter made of poles, brush, and leaves. Later they built a log cabin. They hunted for meat and ate whatever nuts, honey, or wild fruit they found in the woods.

From a young age, Abe helped feed his family by hunting for rabbits and other animals.

The ax was a very important tool for the pioneers. Abe became very skilled at using axes. People would say that if you heard Abe cutting down trees, you would think there were three men at work.

# CHAPTER 2

## The Railsplitter

When Abe was nine years old, his mother died. It was a very sad time for Abe. It was a hard year for him and his sister. They did not have a mother to cook, clean, or make clothes for them. They had to do all the housework themselves.

One year after his mother's death, Abe's father married a woman named Sarah Bush Johnston. She had three children of her own. They all came to live at Abe's house. Sarah was a good mother to them all. She read Abe many books, and she let him go to school as much as possible. He loved to read books like *The Arabian Nights*, *Robinson Crusoe*, and *Aesop's Fables*. He also read books about history and American government. He once said, "Everything I need to know is in books."

During Abe's boyhood, many towns did not have churches. Preachers traveled from one settlement to another to preach.

Abe was popular. He loved to tell jokes and stories. He was also a good listener. He liked listening to preachers giving sermons and lawyers arguing cases. Abe would stand on a stump and speak the way politicians did when they came to town. Everyone would laugh at how Abe imitated people.

By the time Abe was sixteen, he was six feet tall. By the time he was an adult, he was six feet four inches tall. Most men at that time weren't much taller than five feet six inches tall. Abe's bony wrists often stuck out from his shirtsleeves and his ankles stuck out from his pants legs!

As a teenager, he worked from sunrise until sunset. His nickname was the "Railsplitter" because he spent a lot of time using an ax to chop wood into rails for fences. He also spent his time chopping down trees, pulling stumps, and helping clear his father's land. He was lean and strong and his hands were big and powerful. When he was seventeen, he got a job poling a **flatboat** across Anderson Creek, near Troy, Indiana.

In 1828, nineteen-year-old Abe and his friend Allen Gentry built their own flatboat. They loaded it with farm produce and took it to New Orleans for Allen's father. It must have been an exciting trip for Abe. It was the first time he had gone to a big city like New Orleans. It was also the first time he had seen the large slave markets where African men, women, and children were sold at slave **auctions**.

The type of boat Abe first traveled on to get to New Orleans was a flatboat. At the time, the Ohio River was the main route for shipping goods.

Abe was known for being very honest. He once had a job as a store clerk. It is said that, by mistake, he charged a woman too much money for an item in the store. He walked three miles so that he could give her back a few cents of change. The people of New Salem called him "Honest Abe."

14

# CHAPTER 3

## Honest Abe Becomes a Politician

In 1830, the Lincoln family moved to Macon County, Illinois. Abe was now twenty-one years old. He decided he had done enough hard work on the farm. He was now old enough to live on his own. He went to work at a store in New Salem, Illinois.

**As a young man, Abe continued to study and learn whenever he could.**

While he lived in New Salem, Abe joined the New Salem Debating Society. He **debated** men who had gone to college. Abe never went to college. But he was still a fair match against these educated men. He was smart and quick. He spoke well and had interesting ways of making people see his point of view. He studied hard. In 1832, without any experience, he decided to run for a position in the Illinois State Legislature. He was only twenty-three years old.

Abe also joined the militia right away. The state of Illinois was fighting the Black Hawk War. It was a war against Native Americans who were crossing the Mississippi River into Illinois. The United States had taken land from them in 1805. Now people in Illinois feared they wanted to reclaim it.

Black Hawk led the Native Americans in the war against the state of Illinois. Abe spent only two and a half months in the militia. He never saw any battles, though.

**Battle of Bad Axe, ending the Black Hawk War in 1832**

The war did not last long. Abe went back to New Salem. Unfortunately, he lost the **election**. But he promised himself he would run again. He got a job as postmaster and met a lot of people. In 1834, he was ready to try to be elected to the State Legislature once more. This time people remembered the smart young man who gave them their mail. Abe was elected as a **representative**.

Abe went to Vandalia, Illinois, which at the time was the state's capital. He gave speeches and helped pass laws.

Illinois State House in Springfield, Illinois

Abe had a friend from the militia named John Todd Stuart. John was a lawyer, and he let Abe study all his books. Abe became a lawyer, too. He went to work with John in Springfield, Illinois in 1837. Springfield had become the new capital of Illinois. It was an exciting place to work. Abe argued against new states owning slaves.

Pro-slavery rioters burn a print shop in Illinois, 1835.

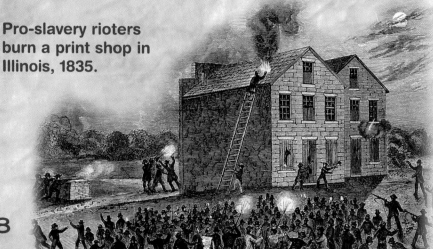

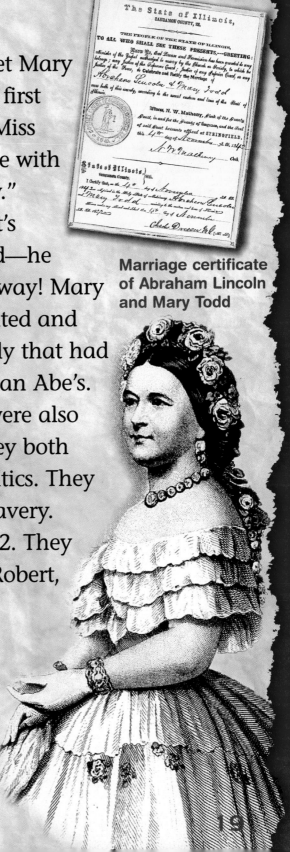

In 1839, Abe met Mary Todd at a dance. His first words to her were, "Miss Todd, I want to dance with you in the worst way." Later, Mary said that's exactly what Abe did—he danced in the worst way! Mary had grown up educated and was raised in a family that had a lot more money than Abe's. But Abe and Mary were also very much alike. They both loved books and politics. They both were against slavery. They married in 1842. They had four children—Robert, Eddie, Willie, and Thomas. Eddie died when he was just four years old.

**Marriage certificate of Abraham Lincoln and Mary Todd**

**Mary Todd had blue-gray eyes and a round, attractive face.**

19

Washington, D.C. from the northeast, 1840s

Abe was elected to go to **Congress** in 1846. He and his family moved to Washington, D.C. Abe wanted to pass a law that ended slavery. People who were in favor of this law were called **abolitionists**. But the law did not pass. Abe was not elected again. Slavery wasn't going to go away overnight.

Abe went back to Springfield with his family to practice law. He joined the 8th **Circuit Court**. It was a court that traveled to small towns on horseback. A lot of towns were too small to have their own lawyers and judges all year-round. Abe and the other court members slept in small inns at night. During the day they heard different cases.

Abe continued to speak out against slavery. He decided to run for **Senate**. Abe ran against a man named Stephen A. Douglas. Douglas believed that individual states could decide whether or not they wanted slavery. Lincoln did not

Lincoln and Douglas debate at Galesburg, Illinois, 1858.

believe any state should be allowed to have slavery. Douglas and Lincoln had many public debates. States in the North didn't want slavery, but states in the South did.

Abe lost the election for Senate, but the debates he had with Douglas made him famous. They were called the **Great Debates**. Everyone had heard of Abe, the tall politician who wanted to end slavery. They remembered him when it came time to vote for a new president.

Abe debated Stephen A. Douglas.

This ambrotype, a type of early photograph, was taken on August 13, 1860, while Abe was running for president.

*"Whenever I hear anyone arguing over slavery, I feel a strong impulse to see it tried on him personally."*

—Speech to 14th Indiana Regiment,

# CHAPTER 4

## A Country Torn in Half

In 1860, the Republican party was happy to have Abe represent them for president. Abe was honored. Election day arrived. Abe won votes from people in the North, but he lost every state in the South. This

Union
Confederacy
Territories

was because the North was against slavery and the South supported it. Abe still had enough votes to be elected president of the United States. But he was only president of half of the country. The United States was breaking apart.

In 1852, Harriet Beecher Stowe wrote a novel called *Uncle Tom's Cabin*. It became a bestseller. It was about slaves who were treated cruelly by their masters. After people read the novel, they wanted to end slavery more than ever.

Harriet Beecher Stowe

23

The states in the South elected their own president. They did not want to be part of the United States any longer. They did not want to be part of a country where Abe was president. They did not want to end slavery. They called themselves the **Confederacy**. The North was called the **Union**. How could Abe make the South join the nation again? After the Confederacy bombed Fort Sumter, a Union fort in South Carolina, Abe sent soldiers to the South. The Civil War began.

On July 21, 1861, there was a big battle called the **Battle of Bull Run**. The Union and Confederate soldiers fought near the town of Manassas Junction, Virginia. It was the first major battle of the Civil War. The Union soldiers **outnumbered** the Confederate soldiers. But the Confederates won the battle. Thousands of men were killed or wounded.

Jefferson Davis, who had been a **senator** from Mississippi, was chosen as the South's new president. He once said, "You cannot transform the negro into anything one-tenth as useful or good as what slavery enables them to be."

President Lincoln and Major General John A. McClernand at Antietam on August 3, 1862

A year later, in 1862, there was a second battle at Bull Run. It was another huge **victory** for the Confederate Army. It made Abe realize that the war was not going to be won quickly.

On September 17th, the **Battle of Antietam** took place in Maryland. The Union won the battle, but almost 5,000 men died and more than 20,000 were wounded. Lincoln was always sad during the war. He once said, "I do not think I will ever be glad again."

Bugle and drums from the Civil War

Then on January 1, 1863, Lincoln signed the **Emancipation Proclamation**. It freed slaves in the South. It was the first step in making slaves free everywhere in America. But the South didn't want to set their slaves free, so the war continued.

A United States Army officer explains the duties of freedom to former slaves in Louisiana, 1863.

**The Address at Gettysburg**

The North was still losing, however. Then, the North won two major victories on July 4, 1863. First, Vicksburg, Mississippi, was captured by Union troops. Then the Union won a battle at Gettysburg, Pennsylvania. Later, Abe gave a speech, called the **Gettysburg Address**, at the battle site. It reminded everyone how important and special our government is.

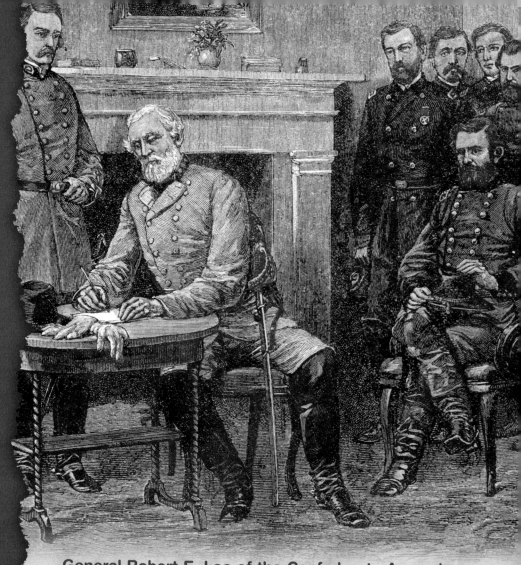

General Robert E. Lee of the Confederate Army signs the surrender at Appomattox to Union Army General Ulysses S. Grant.

In 1864, Abe was elected president for the second time. People from the South were angry, but people from the North knew Abe was helping them win the war. On April 9th, 1865, the South **surrendered**.

Then a terrible thing happened, just five days after the war ended. Mary and Abe decided to go see a play at Ford's Theatre. During the show, a man named John Wilkes Booth shot and killed Abe. Booth did not believe in ending slavery and giving rights to African-American people.

People everywhere cried because a great man had died. Thanks to Abe, slavery was put to an end. A few months after his death, the 13th Amendment was added to the United States Constitution. That meant that all the country's slaves were free.

**Abraham Lincoln's funeral at the White House**

It's been more than 100 years since Abe's death, but we still remember him as one of the country's greatest presidents. A huge marble statue of him sits in Washington, D.C. It's called the Lincoln Memorial. We remember him on a holiday called Presidents' Day. He's remembered in smaller ways, too. Hold a penny in your hand. Take a look at the honest face of the man who became the president of the people and made our country free.

The Lincoln penny was the first American coin to have the face of a president on it. In 1909, President Theodore Roosevelt had an artist design the coin. The smallest coin amount was chosen over a larger coin amount because the penny was the coin of the "plain" people and Abe always said he came from plain folk.

# Glossary

**Abolitionists**: People who wanted to end slavery.

**Amendment**: A change made to a law to improve it, correct it, or add to it.

**Auctions**: Public sales in which things are sold to those who offer the most money.

**Baptist Church**: Church where the members believe in being baptized. Also, its members did not believe in slavery.

**Battle of Antietam** (September 17, 1861): A Civil war battle fought in Maryland.

**Battle of Bull Run** (July 21, 1861): A major Civil War battle fought in Virginia.

**Circuit Court**: A judge and lawyers who travel, holding court in various towns.

**Confederacy**: The group of eleven states that separated from the United States in 1860 and 1861.

**Congress**: The U.S. Senate and the House of Representatives.

**Debated**: To have presented or discussed reasons for and against something.

**Election**: The act of choosing someone by vote.

**Emancipation Proclamation**: An 1863 law signed by Abraham Lincoln that freed slaves in America.

**Flatboat**: A riverboat, usually made of logs, with a flat bottom. It was propelled forward by a pole that was used to push against the river's bottom.

**Gettysburg Address**: Famous speech given by Abraham Lincoln reminding the country how important and special the U.S. government is.

**Great Debates** (1858): A series of debates on slavery that Abraham Lincoln had with Stephen A. Douglas.

**Militia**: Civilians trained as soldiers but not part of the regular army.

**Outnumbered**: To be greater than in number.

**Representative**: A person who is chosen to represent and stand for others.

**Republican Party**: One of two major political parties in the United States.

**Senate**: One part of the legislative branch of the United States government. Each state elects two members, or Senators, into the Senate.

**Senator**: A member of the Senate who is elected to represent his or her home state.

**Slave**: A person owned by someone else.

**Slavery**: The act of owning people.

**State Legislature**: A body of people with the power to make and change laws.

**Surrendered**: To have given up fighting, often unwillingly.

**Union**: The United States during the Civil War.

**Victory**: The defeat of an enemy.